C000072155

MASCULINITY

POETRY

New Chatto Poets II (a contributor)
A Scottish Assembly
Sharawaggi (with W. N. Herbert)
Other Tongues: Young Scottish Poets in English, Scots and Gaelic (editor)
Talkies

LITERARY CRITICISM
The Savage and the City in the Work of T. S. Eliot
Devolving English Literature
Identifying Poets: Self and Territory in Twentieth-Century Poetry
About Edwin Morgan (co-editor with Hamish Whyte)
The Arts of Alasdair Gray (co-editor with Thom Nairn)
Reading Douglas Dunn (co-editor with David Kinloch)
Liz Lochhead's Voices (co-editor with Anne Varty)
Literature in Twentieth-Century Scotland: A Select Bibliography
Talking Verse (co-editor with Henry Hart, David Kinloch, Richard Price)

MASCULINITY

Robert Crawford

CAPE POETRY

First published 1996

1 3 5 7 9 10 8 6 4 2

© Robert Crawford 1996

Robert Crawford has asserted his right
under the Copyright, Designs and Patents Act, 1988
to be identified as the author of this work

First published in the United Kingdom in 1996 by
Jonathan Cape
Random House, 20 Vauxhall Bridge Road, London SW1V 2SA

Random House Australia (Pty) Limited
20 Alfred Street, Milsons Point, Sydney,
New South Wales 2061, Australia

Random House New Zealand Limited
18 Poland Road, Glenfield,
Auckland 10, New Zealand

Random House South Africa (Pty) Limited
PO Box 337, Bergvlei, South Africa

Random House UK Limited Reg. No. 954009

A CIP catalogue record for this book
is available from the British Library

ISBN 0–224–04371–4

Printed in Great Britain by
Mackays of Chatham PLC
Chatham, Kent

for Alice and Lewis

with love

ACKNOWLEDGEMENTS

Acknowledgements are due to the following: *Independent, London Quarterly, London Review of Books, New Writing 2* (British Council), *New Writing Scotland, New Yorker, Observer, Oxford Poetry, Poetry Review, Quadrant* (Australia), *Scotsman, Southern Review, The Sunday Times, Times Literary Supplement, The Wide Skirt.* 'Scotch Broth' formed part of my film *Wurd,* directed by Ken Neil for Scottish Television in 1993.

NOTE

I imagine the refrain in the poem 'Chaps' first of all yelled in an upper-class English voice – 'CHEPS!' – then spoken in a Scottish voice in the middle of the poem, then falling to a whisper at the end.

CONTENTS

Many Happy Returns

MASCULINITY

A QUIET MAN

My best friend at school, then at university
Turned out to be gay

Which was fine, but left me somehow
Lonely. I knew I'd never

Be a ladies' man, or a man's man either.
Unpubby, hating cigarette smoke,

I took out girls to the Art Galleries,
Typing them sonnets. I mooned,

Living in fear some reintroduced
National Service sergeant major

Would noisily break me in two.
Odd those sergeant majors now

Are gender fossils, and here I am
Washing the dishes but not doing ironing,

Married. Evolved from my all-male school
And that bristling, women-only college

I lived in later for years,
I stand off-balance, mumbling something

About our wee son's future, his stripy flag
A dishtowel my Dad brandished when he made me

Like him an in-between, quiet man,
Homo silens, a missing link.

CHAPS

With his Bible, his Burns, his brose and his baps
Colonel John Buchan is one of the chaps,
With his mother, his mowser, his mauser, his maps,
Winston S. Churchill is one of the chaps.

Chaps chaps chaps chaps
Chaps chaps chaps chaps

Rebecca Mphalele is one of the chaps,
Ezekiel Ng is one of the chaps,
Queenie Macfadzean is one of the chaps,
Kayode Nimgaonkar is one of the chaps.

Chaps chaps chaps chaps
Chaps chaps chaps chaps

Oxfordy chaps, Cambridgey chaps,
Glasgowy chaps, Harrovian chaps,
Oxfordy chaps, Cambridgey chaps,
Oxfordy chaps, Cambridgey chaps.

Chaps chaps chaps chaps
Chaps chaps chaps chaps

The sergeant's a chap, the rifle's a chap,
The veldt is a chap, the heather's a chap,
A great JCR of them tossing their caps
Like schoolboys at Eton dyed red on the maps.

Chaps chaps chaps chaps
Chaps chaps chaps chaps

The porthole's a chap, the cannon's a chap,
The Haigs and the Slessors, the Parks are all chaps,
Mungos and Maries, filling the gaps
In the Empire's red line that can never collapse.

Chaps chaps chaps chaps
Chaps chaps chaps chaps

Lord Kitchener needs them to pose for his snaps
Of Ypres and Verdun with chaps' heads in their laps
Singing Gilbert and Sullivan or outlining traps
To catch rowdies at Eights Week, next year perhaps.

Chaps chaps chaps chaps
Chaps chaps chaps chaps

The war memorial's a chap, the codebook's a chap,
The wind is a chap, the horse is a chap
The knitters, the padres, the limbs are all chaps
From Hawick and Africa, poppies are chaps

Chaps chaps chaps chaps
Chaps chaps chaps chaps

NAME AND ADDRESS SUPPLIED

My Edwardian friend Arthur Farquharson
Lived in college three enormous years
With his ties, shirts, trousers, jackets,
Underwear and socks all neatly sporting
An embroidered label, ARTHUR FARQUHARSON,
Then the college address and postcode.
Six months into his college residence
His case was stolen. The hopeful thief,
Finding no lap-tops, cash, or videos,
Just unironed shirts and old school ties,
Beery sportsjackets, Henry Tudor longjohns,
And Scott of the Antarctic vests,
Hurled the slashed suitcase in a shot-putter's arc
Over the windswept, flooded field
Just off the ringroad, so Arthur's most intimate whites
Fell among nettles, a cross between rumpled snowflakes
And parachutists dropped at Arnhem.
Four months afterwards tall, po-faced
Students would amble into the college
With a plastic bag of Arthur's smalls
All birdshit and sodden cotton,
Harvested from scrubland or gutters or animals' burrows,
Then when Arthur slunk back from work each evening
Weary and keeping close to the wall,
The alert porter stood in reception
Brandishing a pair of weathered, just recognisable
Fridtjof Nansen Patent Hyperthermals,
Thundering into the mellow evening
With its arm-in-arm couples, its cricket elevens,
'Mr Farquharson, surely these must be yours?'
    I mention this because once my mother
In a bout of implacable maternal pride
Labelled every piece of my clothing

ROBERT CRAWFORD, HOLYWELL MANOR

And though I haven't lived for years
In that graduate centre, I still get up
On anxious mornings, peering inside
Old socks and cardigans in bleached midwinter
To see what exactly they say.

MASCULINITY

At our school sexes were colour-coded
Blue for a boy and blue for a girl;
A different shade, though, more skyish
On the soft, hard woollen blazer.

Evenings we'd lie up in our rooms
Learning masc. and fem. declensions,
Mensa, mensae. Our diningroom table
Had squat, chunky, rebarbative legs

Unlike those of my lithe first girlfriend
Who crossed hers when she came to tea.
That term I became her Latin lover,
My whole world zinging with testostericity,

All I touched shocked by another language –
Trees, ships, houses, horses, roads
Masculine or feminine, caressed
And confused, the way next term Greek

Gendered things just a little differently,
Maybe because it was older.
It took me years to understand
Erotic grammar and the answer given

By the boy at the back who raised his hand
Erect as a spear, 'Please, sir, please,
Masculinity's not much to do
With sex. It's all about gender.'

GYM

Here they are again: men who are ill-at-ease
In rooms without wallbars or white lines painted on the
  floor,

Press-up counters, peerers into scrums.
They have unlived their coronaries and emphysema

To stand as they did twenty years ago
Erect when they yelled in the gym,

Except now they bawl something different,
Just as stentorian, as devastatingly hoarse,

'Crawford, if ye huvnae learned by now
Masculeenity's a social construct,

Ye're a Great Big Jessie.'
Hanging upside down by his legs,

Bull Roy Jefferies, forehead so stamped on
By rugby-boot studs it's pitted like a solitaire board,

Watches a video of early Germaine Greer.
Mighty Mouse, awarder of a thousand penalties,

Hulks beside him in a WHA'S LIKE US apron
Stirring a wee pan of soup.

When I edge closer it smells not of sweat,
Urine and unshowered Number Eights,

But of minestrone. If only I'd seen him like this
I'd never have demonised him all through boyhood.

I'd have treated him more like a man.

MENDING THE HELICOPTER

I'm too busy mending the helicopter
To wash up yesterday's dishes.

I'm too busy mending the helicopter
To pick up the kids from school.

I'm too busy mending the helicopter
To talk to your doctor about my cigarettes.

I'm too busy mending the helicopter.
I'll have to work through the night with arc lights.

Who do you think I'm mending this helicopter *for*?

REPLY

I've already mended the helicopter.
Leave those rotorblade sprockets alone.

I've already mended the helicopter
While you were watching *Apocalypse Now.*

I've already mended the helicopter.
It needed mending. Radar was a terrible mess.

I've already mended the helicopter.
Why are you out there at night on the lawn

Taking the whole thing to bits?

P C

Interviewed as a New Man Poet
By a sharpsuited journalist in half-rim specs

With blue, constabular eyes,
I'm asked, 'Well, Robert, when was the last

Time you washed the bathroom floor?
And do you have a plan to keep Family Time

Always ring-fenced in your busy lifestyle?'
She scans the livingroom. 'Tell me, Robert,

When it comes to choosing contraceptives . . .'
Fortunately, perched beside me

On this tiny, two-seater settee
Is my legal adviser, a dead ringer

For Sharon Stone in the uncut version
Of *Basic Instinct*. She interrupts smilingly,

'Dr Crawford is making no comment.'

STAR TREK EPIGRAMS

1.

'Mr Sulu, set the controls
To Economy Wash. We're about to venture
Where no man has gone before.'

2.

Kirk to Enterprise: 'I'm going back to my cabin
With a box of Kleenex. I want to experience
The loneliness of command.'

3.

All crewmen report to the foredeck
For Mr Spock's lecture on masculinity,
'Getting in Touch with Emotion'.

RINGMASTER

I was groomed by Aldeboran Huxwin,
Huxquith's grandson. Application form —

Surname: Public School:
   Oxbridge College:
I got the lot right. Huxwin was a publisher

Concentrating on family history.
My job was cross-referencing — '(See under INCOMES)',

'(See under BLACK SHEEP)', '(See under LOW SPERM
   COUNT)'.
I speculated. Matchmaking retrospectively,

I rewired *Debrett's* while Aldeboran whisked off reviewers,
Mostly related by fagging, or money, or lunch.

Left with proofs of *The Origin of Stephens*
Or *England, My Family* marked up in blood-blue ink,

I computerised the family business,
Adding a virus that every month snuck two chaps

From Rangers and Celtic under-21s
Into the House of Windsor,

But I caught that virus. Lonely, with memory lapses,
Pining from bridalwhite NHS sheets,

I hallucinated weddings through my ward-sister's frosted
   glass.
Bridesmaids hacked into the Registrar's computer.

My cake had a title. Waltzing like a honeymoon sperm
Aldeboran blew rings from a twinkling firstclass cigar.

MALE INFERTILITY

Slouched there in the Aston Martin
On its abattoir of upholstery

He escapes
To the storming of the undersea missile silo,

The satellite rescue, the hydrofoil
That hits the beach, becoming a car

With Q's amazing state-of-the-art,
State-of-the-art, state-of-the-art . . .

Suddenly he has this vision
Of a sperm in a boyhood sex-ed film

As a speargun-carrying, tadpole-flippered frogman
Whose visor fills up with tears,

And of living forever in a dinnerjacket
Fussier and fussier about what to drink,

Always, 'Shaken, not stirred.'
Chlorine-blue bikinis, roulette tables, waterskiing –

Show me that scene in *Thunderball*
Where James Bond changes a nappy.

GROWING

THE SECOND WORLD WAR

I was quite close to it, but not yet born.
I was my parents' ration of children,

Saved for through Clydelong, greyish years
Of nissen huts and blacked-out windows.

My family was the calm after that storm:
Miss Millar on the night of the Clydebank Blitz

Picking brambles, coming home to a gapsite;
My bank-teller mother remembering excitedly

Jazz-playing GIs with shining teeth
Queueing in Greenock for Scottish banknotes.

For me their war had a classical soundtrack,
Far, cartoon explosions; a beginning, middle, and end

That lived happily ever after. Dad
Joked about his commando training, his D-Day oath

Never to sleep without a hot-water bottle.
In his pre-war photos he was skinny. He looked like me.

RIPENING

My mother buys my dad a new tweed jacket
Very rarely, always at the sales.

Upstairs in one of two mahogany wardrobes
He hangs it like a shot bird to be cured,

New for a decade, it takes on the smell
Of jackets round it, his scent, the reek of mothballs.

On coathangers, suspended in the dark,
Herringbone accepts the gift of waiting.

Unseasoned pockets sense how ripened pockets
Unfold receipts and stones, then yield up string.

As they get worn, my mother schools thinned elbows
In leather patches, and younger jackets learn

To renounce fashion long before he wears them.
'Is that a new jacket?' 'Yes,' he says, 'it is.'

US

Silence parked there like a limousine;
We had no garage and we had no car.

Dad polished shoes, boiled kettles for hot-water bottles,
And mother made pancakes, casseroles, lentil soup

On her New World cooker, its blue and cream
Obsolete before I was born.

I was a late, only child, campaigning
For 33 r.p.m. records.

Dad brought food parcels from City Bakeries
In crisp brown paper, tightly bound with string.

So many times he felt annoyed
When a visitor left without shutting the gate.

Now someone will bid for, then clear these rooms,
Stripping them of us. We were that floral wallpaper,

That stuck serving-hatch, radiograms polished and broken,
Dogeared carpet-tiles that understood us,

Our locked bureau, crammed with ourselves.

SPIRIT COUNTRY

Over a long Bank Holiday weekend
Letters mature in dark insides of pillarboxes.
On the familiar stroll home from the box
Senders insert an extra sentence,
Alter a promise or the name of an addressee.
Cambuslang, Cambuslang

Where bedroom scenes are protected by sandstone
Villas set well back from the road
Among firs with cones the size of pint glasses,
Sycamores, monkey-puzzles,
Lilacs, broom bushes, self-sufficient redcurrants,
Cambuslang, Cambuslang

Where everyone except blood relations
In Canada, South Africa, or Greenock
Was so local on that dark afternoon
When I knelt down to crayon my first Christmas cards
They needed no stamps above the addresses,
Cambuslang, Cambuslang.

As I walked through the snow to deliver them,
Climbing the steep path at 22 Brownside Road,
I crossed a front garden lit by cold yellow rectangles,
Light-shadows thrown from the livingroom windows
Where the McNeills sat chatting, curtains not yet drawn,
Cambuslang, Cambuslang.

A teenager, I had to imagine
Our left-bank-of-the-Clyde photographers' studios,
Bortsch-specked carpets in the foyer of our Polish Theatre,
Our Art Gallery, our sandstone Opera House,
Our reopened cinema, our Tourist Office, our tourists,
Cambuslang, Cambuslang.

Instead, we had a children's library,
Eight nearby churches, an annual Flower Show
In Cambuslang Institute with miniature gardens
Laid out on tea-trays, their six-inch garden paths
Gravelled with lentils, shrubbery sprigs of parsley,
Cambuslang, Cambuslang

In bonsai form, mum's handbag mirror
Forming still water on an ornamental pond,
Pallisade fencing of old ice-lolly sticks,
A fantasy summerhouse tiled with melon seeds.
I won cups for those gardens on trays,
Cambuslang, Cambuslang

Whose high tea ceremonies governed a suburban cuisine
Of digestive biscuits, Cream Crackers, Jaffa Cakes
Expensive as doilies, in a serviette culture
Rich in shortbread and clean tablecloths'
Ancestral napkins married to napkin rings,
Cambuslang, Cambuslang

Whose leaves were pre-decimal, every bike a Raleigh
Insulated with privet. I visited
By prior appointment short ladies in Central Avenue
Whose dark-varnished lounges denied the post-War world.
Frail and marginal, they pronounced proudly
    'Kembusleng'.
Cambuslang, Cambuslang,

Ha-ha Harry Lauder had lived once in Hamilton Drive
Where but-and-ben bungalows looked built to house
His bakelite songs still lying fragile
In a big, black doctor's bag of records
On our front-room lino near Fingal's Cave,
Cambuslang, Cambuslang,

From Mendelssohn's Hebrides, Handel's Largo,
The Arrival of the Queen of Sheba;
When she came I would watch her progress
Through long-sashed front windows, her trousers brighter
Than any of our curtains. She'd soon be here,
Cambuslang, Cambuslang,

From East Kilbride to carry me away
From my pals with their tricycles and Scalextric sets,
Genesis and Status Quo,
Who suddenly now are living in Cairo
And whose fathers have collapsed like a trellis.
Cambuslang, Cambuslang,

She is coming to carry me off from the bogey
I was always about to plummet on down Douglas Drive.
Somehow none of my friends can compete
With her intellect or vagina.
I'm walking to marry her, in a dark blue suit,
Cambuslang, Cambuslang,

Through a guard of honour of wee white antirrhinums.
I shake hands solemnly with Alan Breck Stewart,
Robert Bruce, Richard Coeur de Lion,
Robin Hood, Biggles, the crew of HMS Ulysses.
I bow low, then stride through the sandstone, whispering
Cambuslang, Cambuslang.

POCKET MONEY

Mealtimes were regular as matins, vespers.
The hours of the day maintained perfect attendance

At our dark-wood wallclock pendent in the hall.
Everything flowed steadily, flower borders, weather

Into its next occurrence, Sunday School
Building each lesson vaguely on the last.

My parents' lives, sealed-unit double glazing,
Though not so modern, looked across suburban

Hedges and monkey-puzzles, sacred spaces
In which you could be sure of meeting no one.

I ran to the railway fields. Unsold-off, free,
They grew dirty mags and dens where me and my pals

Hunkered, watching on a television
Made of old radio valves and bits of tree

Black-and-white Hitler, engine-droning Japs,
Sometimes with interference from the Beatles

Thrumming through Jenny's or Fiona's postered bedroom
In our Sixties semi's walled-off other half.

BOVRILISM

Tramping around as a corduroy student
I was always about to begin The Next Movement in Art.

True, my paintings were pretty sub-
The Scottish Colourists of the 1920s,

But, excitingly, in that dragged brushstroke
Or that stipple, I could see the point

From which in my next-but-one canvas
A new departure might depart.

Now I concentrate on mortgagism,
Dabbling a bit in tinted stuff

Whose varnishy, soulful burnt umbers
Seem somehow, well, *bovriliste*.

THE UMBRELLA STAND

The eroticism of hand-knitted cardigans,
Shower caps and overshoes, wee earthenware pigs
Just to take the chill off the sheets

Dogs me: endearments of freely given
Potatoes and turnips, summer fruits,
Heinz 57, Milk Tray.

Sex was changing in a neuk in the rocks
Carefully into a one-piece bathing suit
On the edge of a cool, sunny ocean.

Sometimes at my parents' house I search
For that alert, tweed-flecky light in their eyes
Through which I came to exist.

NE'ERDAY

Turns out this man at my neighbour's on Hogmanay
Was married to his first wife fifty years ago
By my grandfather whom I never knew.

'Your grandpa, he was a real character;
Took an enormous dram at our wedding.
Exact same name as yourself.'

Suddenly, it's as if I've been granted
A 10p Ne'erday call to the dead
And neither party knows quite what to say

Except that it's marvellous the line's so clear.
He could be standing right here in this room
As the old year goes into the next.

THE MOVE

For forty years they haven't moved house.
Removal men hoist wardrobes out,
Peeling shadows from the walls.

Hard to sell this big, old place,
Unmodernised, uncentrally heated.

They analysed everyone who came to view,
The ones who stayed for a cup of tea,
Or wore wedding rings, or smiled.

My parents seem exhausted, as if their lives
Might never come back from storage,

All their stuff in a warehouse somewhere,
Manhandled, professionally packed.
Staying with friends for six weeks, they're confused

By electric kettles, breadmaking machines,
Food that has to be defrosted,

Then they move into our old house,
Eating off a cardtable, their dining table
Lost somehow in the move.

They look tired. I give them forms to fill in –
Council tax, bus passes, gas.

Gradually they unbox their other life
Into this house, the one Dad, speaking to me,
Calls 'your house', although we've moved.

At first when I walk to visit them
Just up the road, I feel like I did

Going back to the house I grew up in,
Belonging there, then leaving for home.

SCOTCH BROTH

SCOTCH BROTH

A soup so thick you could shake its hand
And stroll with it before dinner.

The face rising to its surface,
A rayfish waiting to be stroked,

Is the pustular, eat-me face of a crofter,
Turnipocephalic, white-haired.

Accepting all comers, it's still our nation's
Flagsoup, sip-soup; sip, sip, sip

At this other scotch made with mutton
That intoxicates only

With peas and potatoes, chewy uists of meat.
All races breathe over our bowl,

Inhaling Inverness and Rutherglen,
Waiting for a big, teuchtery face

To compose itself from carrots and barley
Rising up towards the spoon.

LOCHS

We had to learn so much about lochs
As kids, sucking them up through straws,

While round about us other lochs appeared –
Loch Transit gurgling through domestic pipes,

Loch Radiator Coolant, Loch Tear, Loch Soup,
And then the ones we mustn't talk about,

The wee wee lochs in underwear, Loch Sweat
Only dogs drank at, far

Loch Alcoholism, sunny and serene
With just the possibility of rain.

Long, dry books listed them. We skipped
Instead to sipping at Loch You, Loch Me,

Each, we had read, some eighty-odd per cent
Water, joggling as we walked around

Glasgow which, hydraulically speaking,
Was Northern Finland seen from the sharp sky

In which a tiny plane with scientists
Was dropping on each loch its Finnish name.

RECALL

I have recalled the Scottish Parliament
From hatbands and inlaid drawers,

From glazed insides of earthenware teapots,
Corners of greenhouses, tumblers

Where it has lain in session too long,
Not defunct but slurring its speeches

In a bleary, irresolute tirade
Affronting the dignity of the house,

Or else exiled to public transport
For late-night sittings, the trauchled members

Slumped in wee rows either side of the chamber
Girning on home through the rain.

My aunt died, waiting for this recall
In her Balfron cottage. I want her portrait

Hung with those of thousands of others
Who whistled the auld sang toothily under their breath.

Let her be painted full-length, upright
In her anorak, flourishing secateurs.

She knew the MPs in funny wigs
Would return bareheaded after their long recess

To relearn and slowly unlearn themselves,
Walking as if in boyhood and girlhood

They'd just nipped down to the shops for the messages
And taken the winding path back.

THE CELTIC SAINTS

One twirls a shamrock to explain the Trinity, another
Exorcises a sea-serpent;

Coracling everywhere, spinning round
In their offshore dodgems, banging into gales

Near Lismore or Greenland, birled like Celtic knots,
Their journeys are doodled by God, pushing out

From the Hebrides of themselves – their cells
Made of strong skin, like the body

Avoiding the devil, singing endlessly
Into the endless, praising running water

For its non-stop; their medieval Latin
Is light and hymnlike, a Pictish whisper

Taking the form of an Irish wolfhound
That courses the hills from another mirrory loch

Still undiscovered, with its small green island, its ringing
Bronze quadrangular bell.

CARPET

It unfits itself, picks itself up off the floor,
Flexing and arching in an act of love

That shakes off a filing cabinet,
Airlifting an executive princess

Who feels her career swept under, shivers
As the night wind, riffling her papers,

Blows on harder until the carpet
Smuggles her through the simoon.

Drought-stricken faces hallucinate her
In the bare sky above them, erect at her desk,

A cold newsreader, a claims official
Filing in heaven. One child

With a broken, gangrenous elbow
Stares up soundlessly

At something lovely from the magic stories,
A pretty, stockinged, telephoning lady.

One silver paperclip dangles from the carpet's edge.

THE ELGIN MARBLES

Locals of Fochabers, Garmouth, Kingston,
Lhanbryde, Mosstodloch, Urquhart, Cullen,
Keith and Archiestown, Charlestown of Aberlour,
Rothes, Craigellachie, Lossiemouth, Burghead,
Buckie, Portgordon, Rathven, Portnockie, Findochty,

Listen: toast
The Donatellan profile of Provost Aeneas Duff
With his unplugged megaphone; toast
The Winged Victory he invests with the Freedom of
    Moray;
The Lodge Guest House's Phidian doorbell, part

Of the Elgin Marbles with their pipe band, their fish-
    processing plant
Glacial forever; scenes of minor arrests,
School trips, bookselling in a small economy
Jostling with farmtales and thumbed anthropologies of corn.
They've always been here, out in the fields, on buildings,

Jammed between architraves and cushie-doos,
An unopened secret more local than Pluscarden Abbey,
The Cathedral, Littlejohn's Restaurant. From Elgin's
    deciduous woods
Pan your eyes over snowfields where dikes and neaps,
Marble already, though soft, unfixed,

Wait for monumental masons
To caress dried groundsel and tattie shaws
Into grand entablature. Speyside people
In buggies, gliders, and long *Oresteias* of vans
Are pantheon-friendly, cut out for thigh-deep salmon runs

In bas-relief. On other panels
A country fiddler, the Wolf of Badenoch, big-kneed girls
In the town solarium, shooting brakes, the Palmer's Cross,
Ramsay MacDonald's funeral, Baxters soups,
A waterclock, wheelchair races, a quartz watch.

Some claim the marbles once were brightly painted
So you could see St Maelrubha of Applecross
Was wearing a special tartan to convert Keith,
Could pick out the flecks in an osprey's eye, and feel
The berg-blue slabbed Tay in Tugnet Icehouse

Where they carted the river for storage, ready-sliced.
I read in dram four of the Glenmorangie Manuscript
And in the Golden Book of Dalintober
About harsh easterlies and terriers pissing
On sections the council wanted to replace:

Harbours locked solid with drifters, coracles, zulus
Off before dawn past the Bow Fiddle Rock's
Bottle-nosed dolphins; horsewomen who scythe hay
That seeds through carvings, then dance from their sheen
Down Lady Hill, by Braco's Banking House,

In gutting aprons. Corybantic rain
Smears the marbles, snow drifts over them,
Melts them into spate and into whisky
To heat up broken-veined auld biddies,
Then freeze them, an ingested morgue, corroding

Men's flaky cheeks, too crumbly and deid dune.
Sleeper-weary art historians from London
Plowter and peer hard, sure there's nowt up here
But dreich wee streets, the odd fly fisher's tombstone
Tall as its story, Pictish fag-ends, rain

But
   just when the fir-smashing wind ploughs in, above
Eye level, alert as a photo-essay
Are the chimney pots of Elgin, its renascent
Steel-and-glass station, its laughter, its provost's voice
Of a tweed democracy whose conga line

Snatches you so you're joined with this local
That's extra-local, a wee bit fou on its lang
Post-panathenaic gala day
Of PMs, strangers, accents, saintly gardeners
Catching you up. You're part of it. You shout,

'Aberdeen-wower, envy of the people of Brechin!
WE are the Elgin marbles! Come and join!'

THE GAELIC CARIBBEAN

for Fred D'Aguiar

I want the silence to be broken,
Then unbroken, healing around you.

A boat noses into Barra,
Volleyed by the Atlantic, anachronistic.

People are battened in its hold, speaking
Spanish-Gaelic – cleared, aborted

Mixed infants, their parent language
The torn-out tongues of America.

A boat noses into Barra
So shot-up it will stay

Anchored in long stories and heather roots,
A Cree boat, a Nevis boat, a vessel

Filled with everything spilt. Mama Dot
Will croon in Gaelic and Guyanese Gaels

On their plantations of drowsy peat
Unslave themselves to listen.

Cortez is giving way to St Brendan.
All night a woman cries

Something island, a Creole
Clearing word that dismisses the silence

Then whistles it back like a shepherd calling
His lost black dog from the seaweed.

JESUS CHRIST ENDORSES THE NEW HILLMAN IMP

I was in our works canteen when a call
Came over the tannoy to watch him endorse the new car.
As he bent and touched it, he said,
'This product will save your area
For another decade: it will be loved
Equally by US management
And families whom its air-cooled rear engine
Will power to school. I'm saying this
That you may take pride in your work.'
Nervous execs whooshed him away
For a photo session.
                                    I lost my job
In the first redundancies.
'Does the daffodil have an income allocation model?
Will the company keep you safe
In a world downturn? Will you see this factory levelled?'
Hillmans have long gone out of production.
My launch brochures in a box upstairs
With his photo are greeny with damp.
We did good work, though. No regrets.
It was true what he said, standing up
On a platform in Linwood, Scotland,
Endorsing the new Hillman Imp.

INCARNATION

Homes round the kirk are its harled
Acoustic community, thirled to the dialect Word

Thrawn at the roots of platinum blondes, inveigling
Between hinge and door-jamb, an insidious Christ of petrol,

Scuffed shoes and farmdogs, his rich kenotic bread
Wrapped on the shelves of rural supermarkets,

His frogspawn jamjarred from ponds:
Til him at hes mair will be gien,

Christ of 'The Cottar's Saturday Night',
Doctor Who and CDs,

Out there at the edge of the snowfields
In his overalls, sniffing, listening for something,

Then scliffing back into the village,
Dry-eyed, ready to eat.

THE PENGUIN SAINTS

I think of the great Bovril-drinking saints
At their altars, in their eventide homes,

Of whom little is known – St Gwinear (?sixth century),
Elizabeth Seton, the first American saint,

Married to a professor of anatomy;
The three St Ivos, the three St Pelagias,

Each arriving, just like us,
In a world without enough names,

Then being bundled into a list
Where they all look holy, all the same,

Rows of bungalows on bourgeois avenues,
Hairs of the head; sparrows.

THE NUMTIES

The parsnip Numties: I was a teenager then,
Collecting clip-together models
Of historical windsocks, dancing the Cumbernauld bump.

Satirical pornography, plant-staplers, nostalgiaform shoes
Were brochure-fresh. It was numty-four
I first saw a neighbour laughing in a herbal shirt.

Moshtensky, Garvin, Manda Sharry –
Names as quintessentially Numties
As Hearers and Bonders, duckponding, or getting a job

In eradication. Everything so familiar and sandwiched
Between the pre-Numties and the debouch of decades after.
I keep plunging down to the wreck

Of the submerged Numties, every year
Bringing back something jubilantly pristine,
Deeper drowned, clutching my breath.

HEEPOCONDRY

Ech ma buffets, ma heavit kirnels,
Ech, ech, Ah'm fair poostit,
That swarfin wi swalms, ech, torflin
An aye peesie-weesie, misthriven. Ah cannae
Tak a drabble of chiffin, ech.
Ah thratch an Ah traik. Ah'm aye oorie.
Doactir, doactir, ech,
Doactir.
(Yon doactir disnae unnerstaun.)

NEXT

Count the trees on Prince Edward Island;
Set the economy to rights;
Give birth; meet the new sales targets;
Eat more fresh vegetables; work nights.

Quote the corporate mission statement
At dinner parties; shave on the phone;
Eavesdrop on the unemployment figures
Late at night and on your own.

Squeeze your eczema; squeeze your mortgage;
Squeeze your pillow to make it choke
And give in, telling you you've made it;
Stare at the squat alarm clock

As it bleeps and bleeps and you count each bleep
Over and over and over again,
As if waking up were a sleep technique,
A kind of committee-meeting Zen.

Re-count the trees on Prince Edward Island;
The manager says you go them wrong.
Spruce and Scots firs and apple orchards:
The manager says you got them wrong.

CONSUMPTIVE

I sing the market economy, empowering bicycles and
  nasturtiums
Through share interactions, tungsten and unusual
  sponsorship.
What does the swallow or the Bugatti know of tariff
  barriers?
I sing the improved safety record of offshore industrial
  workers, brides,
And machinists everywhere, tooling elm legs for chairs.
I paean the mutuality of agreements, inventiveness,
  corporate raiding.
I overflow with the credit system's efficiency, smart cards
  and modems
Allowing global movement of artificial limbs
To meet projected requirements. I give thanks for software
  specialists
In service and retail, tourism, cultural industries.
I adore transnational corporations,
Pray for group loyalties, proactive spirituality
Incarnate in crèches, hairdressing, mortgage protection
  schemes.
Education increasingly I hymn, MBAs
Replacing Sanskrit, fast-track financial reporting
In electronic and print media; I exhort you, new
  democracies,
Rise and participate in income generation
Like there's no tomorrow, or tomorrow will last just six
  hours.
Buyouts, share-issues, enterprise initiative schemes,
You are the economy's bulwark – conduct yourselves with
  pride.
Privatisation thrills me, I revel in publicity shots
Of heroic loaves and joky lager commercials.

Demand me. For a limited period only
Now out of sycophantic respect
For you, the enjoyers of all these goods,
I invite you to invest in this song.

AUTOCUE

Leathery feet, metrical psalms
Jammed into unidiomatic
Purposeful English
Float up on autocue

In choppy lines,
The earth belongs
Unto the Lord
And all that it

Contains –
Streets, adverts, cars,
An ambulance's
Hyperventilating strobe

As words scroll up
I'm fed
This intimate script,
Ye gates lift up

Your heads on high
Ye doors
That last for aye;
When I go fast

So does the cue,
And when I drag
It slows its pace
In front of me

Each word-processed
Accompanying word
Bringing bloodslicks too, the felt-
Pen geniality of Christ.

BALLAD

Taper, baby's penis,
Smoke billowing into the dark,

You make a scliff of light on helmets,
An eerie skimming of wings.

At Maes Howe or Dunfermline
Ballantrae or Cowdenbeath

You're the other of the twa corbies,
A coin flung into a well,

Bouncing over its mossy lip,
Making that emptiness flicker.

TWO-LINE POEM

on the centenary of the West Highland Line
for Wilson, Mary, and Joe

The first line starts with Glasgow, ends with Oban,
But the second breaks off, longer, more involved

With bog and dynamite. It sets down porters
At unmanned stations, returns to signalboxes

Sly engineers who built them, till it stops
With its origin – a low-paid army

Letting off steam: a lost legion of navvies
Pouring out their Roman aquaduct

At the head of Loch Shiel so we could sail along it
On rails that shone like water, speeding up

To our Railway Camping Coach at Morar station,
My father's hand trying not to break the mantle

When he lights the gas lamps and we go
To bed, three extra sleepers on that siding.

Past Polnish schoolhouse where the Rosses waved
Lochailort platform's rucksacked with our friends

Who picnic with us, pouring tomato soup
From a tartan flask. Some wear

The uniforms of the old North British Railway,
Others have Seventies sci-fi Nehru jackets

Or are unborn, but all are pulled by engines
Waiting at red lights to pass one another

On the single track. Today at Arisaig
An Edwardian telegraphist rattles down her window to
    speak,

Then the whistle goes and our two long trains snake out
In opposite directions – future, past –

But this evening and every other evening
These two will pass again, almost on time.

LA MER

Is that a bathing cap or a seal's head
Surfacing in the 1930s?

This morning the sea does a huge baking
Of scones and fresh apple tart,

Mixed up with herring, cod and shrimps,
Cuttlefish, fruits de mer.

The sea clears everything away
To set a fresh place. It repeats itself

Like Alzheimer's Disease.
Its moony rollers cast me ashore –

A creel, a fishbox from Crail or Vilnius,
A piece of boat, old but ready

To be put to some startling re-use.
Voices, phonelines, everything flows:

Dad in his landing-craft, beached
At Normandy, us cruising the Small Isles

In the Seventies, Eigg, Rhum, Muck, Canna
Bobbing up one by one, dark collies

Chasing their tails, retrieving sticks from the breakers,
Mr McConnochie's painting of Aphrodite

Breezing to the Arisaig beach on a clamshell.
When I was wee I knew the music

Was about the sea, but I thought its title
Was a French phrase meaning 'My Mother'.

MANY HAPPY RETURNS

ICEBREAKER

Not sure how to begin, but
Something to do with October light

Bleaching the North Sea, till the horizon
Shines like a floe, chilling my sinus,

While that freighter, bow
Angle-on to me, could smash through

The forget-me-not-coloured Alaskan calm
Just off St Andrews Bay

Where I stand at the railings and new students gawp
At the term's start, eyeing everyone up,

As we did, do, you waiting
Right at the head of the white marble stairs

And me sailing up them, eyes on your hair,
Weighing the very first words.

WINTER

That night we drove to hear about adoption
You jumped an unmarked junction, trying to find
The Social Work Centre. When we did, we sat
Ten minutes in the warm car, then went in.

We were the quietest of all the couples.
The walls were covered in felt-pen drawings, toys
Cluttered the place. Committedly,
A foster-parent told us what that meant

But cold seeped in from black-iced Dundee streets;
Swing-doors blew open; if it snowed, they'd close the
     bridge,
Stranding us there. I couldn't really tell
Just what we wanted. I wanted too much:

Not to feel so old, to be able to believe in luck,
To remember sitting with these other couples
In a semi-circle on bright scatter-cushions
Watching a vid in coats and anoraks.

NORMAL

My psychiatrist was reassuringly normal –
Neither Woody Allen nor Herr Doktor Freud –
More like my non-existent elder brother

Explaining things. Sometimes in the waiting-room,
I'd see another patient: they looked so normal
Like busy people in the supermarket

Pushing their trolleys round with tinned food, papers,
Paying for it all by credit card
At the checkout where the assistant passes barcodes

Across a scanner. Checking signatures,
She smiles at each customer, guessing from their shopping
Which one of them believes she has a soul.

SEAHORSES

At night they fly up from the road's
Cat's-eyes, two fresh splashes of seaweed,

A lovely omen, intertwined
Round the farmtouns of Angus, throwing the North Sea
    in the air,

Floating us deeper into our marriage
With fins and wings, bucking hooves rapping

Horse against horse in eared darkness,
You-me and I-you, there ahead

The dancing seahorses of Aberlemno
Sheheing upright along the night,

Wee dragons, sheltie-haddocks, curled
Round one another, eye to eye,

Take us up into the Angus evening,
Take us up, then plunge us under.

LOGANAIR

Below, a freelance palaeontologist
Gets stuck in with his JCB,

And here, from the winter airspace of Fife,
Coal-dark, nocturnal Burntisland

's drip-painted with streetlamps, the Forth's edge
Scribbled with motorway lights.

You're invisible. I'm fourteen thousand feet up,
Viewing the scan of our unborn child,

Nearing you over the prop-driven landscape,
Its November villages insect wings

Shimmering in carbon, carrying towards you
Cellophaned, machine-readable flowers.

THE HANDSHAKES

I flinched at the handshake of a woman in labour
Through mid-contraction when you pushed our son

Down towards the forceps.
Soon his fingers curled

Possessively around my index finger
And then round yours,

Welcoming us with a reflex action
To take your hand beyond yon Labour Suite

Where you clutched me as you breathed the Entonox
And called for your own mother, who is dead.

CARDIGANS

While you're lying in the post-natal ward
I go into Dundee to Arnott's sale

To buy you cardigans. Fingering the rails
Gets mixed up with the touch and smell of milk

White as the pads of cricketers
In Lochee Park, your afterbirth Spicy Tomato

In that Pizza Hut with a plaque built where the house
Of the Wedderburns once stood, the great town clerks.

I think of them in the queue for the 95
Through Tayport to St Andrews, past cock pheasants

Strutting by rapeseed, rabbits crouched on a football pitch.
I remember softest cotton on your skin

And me this morning buying women's clothing
In Dundee, the city where our son's just born.

WHISHT

Wee towdy mowdy creel, peat wame,
Folic acid bank,
Ye ken the showers tae come, an ken
The pechin, pechin kink

O aa the born glens,
Corbetts an craigs, scamperin
Hutherons an fleckies, streakers, pods
The warld is mam tae, whan yi're great, then green.

WHISPER

Little lovely womb, peaty womb, peat-bank of folic acid,
you know the birthpangs to come, and know the panting,
panting convulsive catching of the breath of all the born
glens, mountains and crags, scampering young heifers and
spotted cows, fast hunting dogs and neat small beasts that the
world is midwife to, when you're big with child, then after
the delivery.

MANY HAPPY RETURNS

Soon it'll be the day I was born.
I'll be where I wasn't: at home with Dad
Who fries up a celebration breakfast,
Anticipating the phonecall.

Bright as long-remembered candles,
Other people fly back too:
Nana, Aunt Jean and Uncle Watt
With presents – big, obsolete coins.

Almost time for my first cry
In the labour ward, my smudgy face
Grimacing and gawping
Just like that of my baby son

Coming to join in the party.
I remember nothing until I was three,
But a nurse is going to telephone,
'Hello, Mr Crawford?' That's me.

EUCALYPTUS

Too near the house, that tree had to come down.
You lay open-mouthed
At the chainsaw's arc of shavings

Sprayed across the window you were held at,
Baptising you before the fat trunk thumped
Into pre-memory. You won't remember

Its blue-grey-green, the leaves' smell after rain,
Yon in Australia-in-St Andrews givenness
Yours before you knew, with your flatpack cot,

Your 0–3 months clothes in plastic bags,
Your chosen name, your mum at eight months pregnant
Walking downstairs so carefully each day.

THE TICKET

We're careful, trying to save – replacement windows,
A flat roof by the North Sea, paying back over

Two thousand pounds non-statutory pay.
Today while I was left holding our baby

You nipped out just to get some Christmas stamps
And got a parking ticket. You came home anxious,

'I shouldn't have chanced it.' Right,
But now I love your tiny criminal record,

Your scar, our tiny needle's-eye of risk.
Blessed are we who slip from moderation

The way our baby girns and scowls and quickly
Just laughs and laughs and laughs out of sheer badness.

THE LOOK-IN

One day when I was skiving off my day-job,
Sitting writing at my black-ash desk

Eyes down, intent, you came and stood outside
The French windows my son likes to look out of

At age six months. You told me later
How you'd stayed a moment, unseen, watching me

At work in this new house, this warm room.
I imagine, Dad,

You leaning on your stick, eighty years old,
Visiting for an instant and then gone.

I want to sit here pressing forward
Into the daydream that's the real work,

My job to know you there and know the knowledge
Doesn't interrupt me, nourishes what I do

Subliminally, not raising my head,
Like someone praying: a seventh sense, an eighth.

BABBY

Pirnie-taed babby,
Yir whorlbanes an trams,
Yir wee spyogs bane o ma bane,

Watchin *Dad's Army* wi yir knaps,
Ee me wi yir hailskinnt unhattered skin
Kennin aathing that's yir ain.

Pirnie-taed – pigeon-toed; babby – baby; whorlbanes – hip-bones or joints; trams – (jocular) legs; spyogs – paws/hands/feet/legs; bane – bone; knaps – kneecaps; ee – eye; hailskint – having an unblemished skin; unhattered – without skin eruptions or sores; kennin – knowing.

THE CRITICISM

I who can't play any instrument,
Whose singing is crap, who was once chucked out of a
    choir

For my utterly expressionless face,
Sing to my baby till his rubbed-at eyelids

Waver. He sprawls in my arms
Not knowing if he's hearing 'The Skye Boat Song',

'Silent Night' or some early Seventies
TV soundtrack. He falls asleep

With a whole-body look of ecstatic boredom,
His breathing in tune with my own.

THE JUDGE

At six months my son sits like a judge
On the High Chairage of Scotland.

His hands rest on a wee shelf in front of him.
He weighs us up. He takes advice from a spoon,

And we crouch, looking on, waiting
Years for a sentence that, when it comes,

Will be reported wise, long-considered,
Irreproachably just.